Joseph Franklin Perry

Principles of dog training, originally

Joseph Franklin Perry

Principles of dog training, originally

ISBN/EAN: 9783337814830

Printed in Europe, USA, Canada, Australia, Japan

Cover: Foto ©ninafisch / pixelio.de

More available books at **www.hansebooks.com**

PRINCIPLES

OF

DOG TRAINING

ORIGINALLY

"DOG PATHS TO SUCCESS"

BY

W. C. PERCY ("KIT KILLBIRD")

CAREFULLY REVISED AND EXTENDED

BY

"ASHMONT"

BOSTON

J. LORING THAYER

1886

PREFACE.

THE basis of this handbook is "Dog Paths to Success," a work on dog training, which appeared a few years since, from the pen of Mr. W. C. Percy, well known to American sportsmen as "Kit Killbird." The merits of the book found immediate recognition, and a rapid sale of the entire edition followed. Appreciating the great demand for it, which remained unsupplied, the copyright was purchased by me from the author. After a thorough revision of the text, and with some important additions, the work, under a new and more euphonious title, is now submitted to the amateur dog trainer, for whom it is designed. No inconsiderable portion of the first edition was deemed extraneous, and therefore omitted. All its practical points of importance have, however, been given special prominence in these pages, and the system of training herein advocated is distinctly the same as that presented by Mr. Percy in his original work.

"ASHMONT."

BOSTON, November, 1886.

CONTENTS.

PRINCIPLES OF DOG TRAINING.

CHAPTER I.

HOW TO HANDLE A DOG.

IF, reader, you are a novice in handling dogs, are impatient, excitable, and easily angered, and you do not feel certain that you can restrain your temper under circumstances more than ordinarily trying, then I would advise you not to undertake the management of a well bred pup. These faults are grievous; their influence upon him would be hurtful, and not impossibly ruinous. You would, therefore, do better to procure for your use a dog already broken, and fixed in habit and character.

The first and most essential attribute in a trainer is a natural affection for his dog, and the indispensable qualifications to ensure success are patience and perseverance. He may unite temper with these qualities, but must not display the

same. If he has it under subjection he is better
qualified to succeed than if he were without it. I
have always observed that men possessed of high
temper, able to restrain it, have more will and
resolution, and are less likely to abandon any
project or enterprise which they undertake. Temper, when under control, becomes a nobler attribute, spirit; but when unrestrained it degenerates
into a beastly passion, deprives man of reason,
strips him of dignity, and places him on a level
with the brute whose standard he will in vain
attempt to elevate.

I would not advise you, as some authorities
have done, to procure a spike collar and attempt
to teach your pupil everything at once. These
men, denouncing the whip as an instrument of
torture, would substitute another doubly severe
in its application, and no more calculated to disa-
buse the mind of the tortured pupil of the instru-
mentality of his master in the punishment.

Though the education of sporting dogs should
begin in early puppyhood, my experience warrants
me in fixing the limit at the fourth month. Lessons begun much earlier than this, I am inclined
to think, beget timidity, unless great caution on

the part of the trainer is used, and I know of no weakness more objectionable in a dog intended for the field or other purpose.

Until the age mentioned, a pup should only be petted, caressed, and fed by the hand of his master. He should be accustomed to accompany him in short walks and rambles, and made to feel at home and easy in his company. He should be familiarized with the roads and paths leading to and from the house, and accustomed to the sight of strangers, different objects and animals about the premises, in order to acquire a sufficient degree of confidence and fearlessness to withstand any distracting agency which may operate against the efforts of the trainer when the hour of instruction arrives. The words "Come in" or "Come here" should be used whenever occasion demands, or when he is approached with his plate, or tidbit reserved for him. These words he soon learns to associate with something which you design for him, be it a kindly stroke or a morsel to eat, and, if repeated often, their intent and purpose soon become fixed in his mind, and he learns to obey promptly. Now, regarding the effects of sights and sounds upon puppies, no close or even casual observer of dogs has failed to notice the difference between the town and the country whelp. The one is generally bold, fearless, and indifferent to everything around him; the other is wide awake to the approach of strangers, his manner shrinking, and his ear pricked at every unusual noise or sound. The latter, however, in the end, develops into the best fielder, because of the easy and ready access to game which the fields near his home afford.

CHAPTER II.

" To fetch " is the very first lesson which
should be taught. I hold that all propensities
and inclinations of a dog which tend to his
ultimate good, and especially those which assist
the trainer, should be assiduously cultivated, and
surely there are none earlier developed than this
desire to run and fetch a ball, a glove, or other
object thrown for his pleasure. Here is where a
pup practically learns the meaning of "fetch,"
which he will never forget when taken out on
game. This practice becomes, as it were, a habit,
and fixed habits in man and beast are second
nature, the power of which maintains its sway
through life. Some trainers advise the deferring
of this branch of a pup's tuition ; then, when it
is commenced, to use the spike collar as the first
means of teaching him to retrieve. I am surprised at their doing this before trying a simpler
and more pleasing plan. It may answer very well

11

for old, hard-headed dogs, the education of which has been neglected; then potent remedies are required, but the application of this instrument to very young dogs is as cruel and unwarrantable a practice as advocates of the whip ever resorted to. I know that I antagonize a few trainers when I denounce the use of the spike collar upon young dogs; nevertheless, I am entitled to a right of opinion, especially when I base it upon personal experience.

The use of the spike emanated with professional breakers, who train and educate dogs for a pecuniary consideration, and whose aim is to attain the end in a given period or as short a time as possible. Their motives are any other than humane, and they are not influenced by that affection for their pupils which true sportsmen naturally possess. Few of us, in our respective spheres, are sufficiently patient. The owner of a dog who expects him to work from a sense of love and attachment, and follow up the course of early impressions, must be content to wait, and should not look for first-class execution before the second season on game; before he can become a thoroughly reliable hunter, in and out of sight, one fully qualified in every branch of the service, still another season of practice will be needed.

Now, as teaching to "fetch" is unattended, or should be, with acts of violence, a pup is admissible to this department of learning at the age of three months, and, if well grown and healthy, even earlier. Commence with him by rolling a ball, or throwing a glove, across the floor. You must sit down, in a position that will induce him to return to you after he goes for the object. When he picks it up, say "Fetch," and caress him if he does so. Use no other word than "Fetch," lest you confuse him. Continue to exercise him twice a day in this manner, during your leisure moments; in three weeks' time you will be pleased* to see how well he obeys, and, at the command "Fetch," looks about in search, even before you have cast the ball or glove for him. Never strike or cuff him when he refuses to come back, or stops to play with his ball, as is often the case. The little rascal will probably roll over, gnaw his plaything, and apparently taunt you with this delay, or, if fatigued, no amount of urging will move him. You must be patient and considerate with him at this age, remembering that he is a mere pup, and not looking as far and anxiously into the future as you are; besides, this is a lesson which you are trying to "steal upon him." You must, therefore, consult his humor, and embrace opportunities when he presents them. The lesson is one which repetition develops into a habit, the force of which will gather strength, and at maturity prove a most essential acquirement. It is a discipline which should be persisted in while yard-breaking, and until the pupil is a year old or more, being omitted only occasionally for two or three weeks at a time, as other lessons are commenced.

Of those who complain of not having time to devote to this exercise, I would ask, what better opportunity could you desire than the long winter nights, when everything is quiet, save, perhaps, the singing of the half-green chunk on the fire, to the inviting glow of which the pup is more than pleased to gain admittance. At just such times and places, with an old stocking or a slipper, has been laid the foundation of many a champion's bright career.

CHAPTER III.

"HEED" — "HIE ON."

SUPPOSING your pup to be four months old, it is high time to teach him one of his most important lessons, viz.: to stand or point at the command "Heed" or "To-ho." The latter term is more commonly taught by English keepers, but I prefer the former, and the majority of sportsmen in the South are accustomed to it. It is a monosyllable, and easily spoken, it is a more expressive word and, therefore, to be preferred. This lesson may be begun with the aid of a piece of beef or biscuit, or his plate of dinner, either of which, when placed before your puppy, he will naturally evince an eagerness to obtain. You must restrain him by putting your open hand under his throat; firmly hold him back, and at the same time say "Heed." Stroke him on the back with the free hand, repeating the command, "Heed," then release him suddenly and say "Hie on!" After he has eaten his morsel, put down

15

another, over which he will be as frantic as before, and, finding himself again restrained, will attempt to dodge his head under your wrist. Hold him back firmly, but kindly, and repeat the command " Heed " several times, before releasing him to the order " Hie on." Repeat the lesson frequently during the day, and always at meal-times. Never permit him to eat without this restraint upon his eagerness, and in a few days you will see that he is beginning to associate the command " Heed " with the act of stopping, and " Hie on " with that of going forward. Then, in order to make him obey without holding, tap him lightly on the head when he appears too eager, and say " Heed." In this way, he will soon learn to stand and patiently wait the order " Hie on." Continue this practice for several days; in all probability, you will then be able, while several feet from your dog, to make him hold his position, and advance at the word of command.

You must be patient and forbearing; do not attempt too much, or severely test your pupil's mental capacity. Remember to give but one lesson at a time, for a term of days or weeks, in order to impress it indelibly on the mind. Only when that one has been well learned should another be commenced. The check cord is sometimes employed by the trainer, and is an admirable auxiliary agent upon very headstrong subjects. When required, it should be attached to the neck or collar, and with the command "Heed," or "To-ho," the dog should be jerked; or, by placing your foot on the end of the cord, the dog be allowed to jerk himself. Now, the jerk and command, coming together simultaneously, will be associated in his untutored mind, and to escape the one, he will be glad to obey the other. As I have never had occasion to use the cord in this lesson, I would not recommend it excepting in extreme cases.

The next step is to take your pup to a close room, or to a secluded spot in the yard, where there is nothing to distract his attention from his lessons. Call him to you, show him a piece of beef or bread, and with a waft of your hand toss it to the right. When he rushes for it, command him first to "Heed"; then, after obeying, to "Hie on." Call him in and try him in the same way on the left. Then take a stone or chip

(something not edible) and a piece of meat, and
throw one to the right, the other to the left, being
sure he sees them both fall. Hie him on, and let
him take his choice of directions; and if, per-
chance, he should go to the corner opposite the
meat, he will draw blank, and then dash across
to the other to find his morsel. This will teach
him to quarter and hunt up his game. After
finding the meat, always whistle him to you.

You will now do well to teach your pup to
come "to heel" when called. You should also
begin to accustom him to remain at your side
during the daily walks which you take with him.
Instead of a chain, a stick about the length of a
cane, or a light cane itself, may be used, and on
the end of this a snap should be fastened. To
the ring of his collar this may be attached, and by
this means he can be kept opposite your legs as
you walk. Apply this restraint for only short
distances at first, and when released bid him "hie
on." After a short time, the attachment can be
dispensed with; you must then be certain that he
does not leave your side until you have signified
your consent by the same words of command.

CHAPTER IV.

" CHARGE."

WHEN you see that he has become quite stanch and obedient, and has reached, we will say, the age of five or six months, you can then begin to teach him to " down charge." This lesson, like every other, is a little difficult at first, but with patience all trouble is soon overcome. Gently force your dog into the desired position, with forepaws extended, and his head stretched out on or between them. Say, at the same time, " Down charge," or " Charge," as you prefer, and repeat the command until he is relieved with " Hie up," or " Hold up." When he attempts to rise before being ordered to do so, tap him on the head, or press on his back, and repeat the command. You must go slowly at first, until he begins to associate the command with his peculiar posture. After a time, as your pupil progresses, you may, using good judgment, become more austere in your manner, and force him to obey promptly at the word. Practise him frequently in this way,

19

and repeat the instructions daily until they are fully understood.

Now, when you have succeeded in making your dog " heed," " hie on," and " charge " promptly (which are the most important branches of his education), and have at intervals continued to exercise him with the glove or ball, there is in order another lesson, which goes further towards bringing a young dog under control, and enabling him to distinguish between the various commands, than any that I have ever seen tried — viz.: calling him off his point. This in the field is not necessary or advisable; but in the yard it teaches him to give ear and attention, and not confound one command with another. Now, supposing a morsel of bread has been thrown him, or there is a tempting plate of dinner, over which he stands or " heeds " when ordered, and you say, " Come here." Having been accustomed to " hie on," he will, of course, rush forward at the first sound of your voice, not knowing that you wish him to " come in," when heretofore at this juncture he has been told to " hie on." You must be ready to cry " Heed " again, and make him stop; then repeat the order, " Come here, sir," and upon his first motion forward, cry "Tut, tut, come here. Come here, sir," repeating these words rapidly to break up the chain of reasoning that is binding him at the moment. When he turns his head to look at you, snap your finger at him, stoop down, and insist upon his coming in. As soon as he obeys, pat him and let him on to his plate. Only two or three trials are required to make him act properly in this work. The dog understands well enough the meaning of "Come here," but he is confused at your commanding him at such a time and place, so contrary to what he has been accustomed to. As soon as he is perfected in this lesson, it will be no little pleasure to observe how attentively he awaits to obey your different orders, never mistaking one for another. After each call from his point, make him "down charge," with his face to the plate. With the expenditure of a little time and some effort, this exercise becomes a very pleasing one; it thoroughly subdues the pup's excessive eagerness, and places him under more complete control.

I have broken braces in this manner, and allowed them to approach within a foot of tempting bits of cooked meat, there to await the command, either "Hie on," or "Come in," which they had learned to distinguish and obey with great accuracy and precision. The sight of two dogs charging promptly together, eying each other jealously, "hieing on" and "coming in" to order, is one that would elicit the admiration of the most indifferent spectator. When a child is made to recite the first lessons in addition which he has committed to memory,— for instance, one and one are two, one and two are three, and so on, — how readily he answers, and smilingly rejoices over his accomplishment; but pray observe his astonishment and confusion when the question is put to him out of the order as given in his book, or as he has been taught. The exercise is not unlike the one I have just recommended for the canine pupil, and there is none which serves to rivet the attention more firmly, or assists him more to distinguish, as I said before, the significance of the various commands without mistaking one for another. When your dog is perfectly familiar with the preceding lessons, he should be practised in various ways and on different grounds, where the terms, the meaning of which has been taught him, are applicable.

CHAPTER V.

WHEN the exercises are varied, as is plain to be seen, unusual experiences will be encountered. Although the use of the same terms of command already taught him will be needed, change is salutary, relieving the monotony of the young dog's routine, and thereby conducing to the strength and vigor of his reasoning powers. The following practice has aided me much in perfecting my own dogs; I would, therefore, advise others to follow it.

Take three or four short stakes, or pieces of picket lumber, about two and one-half feet long; sharpen one end, and drive them into the ground to the depth of six or eight inches; they should be in a line, and about twenty feet apart. On the top of each, nail a small piece of board or plank about six or eight inches square, large enough, at least, to hold a bit of meat or bread. After you have arranged them, step off a short

23

distance, call the pup, show him a piece of meat in your hand; then make him "down charge," and remain so while you go forward and put it on the top of the nearest stake. Now come back to him, and hie him on, making him heed, or to-ho, when within a few feet of the stake. After he is ordered on and allowed to take the meat, call him in; then make him "down charge," and remain in that position while you go forward again. Walk down the line and put your hand on all the stakes, in the manner of children's play of "Hide the Thimble"; this time leave the meat on the last stake in the row. When you return and hie your dog on, of course he will go to the first stake, where he was so fortunate before; but not finding his prize, after nosing around the foot of the stake and mounting to the top again, he will dash off to the next stake, and so on down the row, until he at last discovers the object of his search. After you have exercised him in this manner for a few days, you can add more stakes and place them about promiscuously, thereby prolonging his search and making it more difficult for him to find his coveted morsel. When he seems confused, encourage him with the words "Hunt for it"; this teaches him to range and feel close with his sensitive nose.

In this exercise, the dog should always be thrown off to windward ; and if the meat that is used to tempt him has been placed on the coals for a minute or so, he will not give up the search as long as he sniffs the enticing odor. No method of yard-training is better calculated than this one to bring a dog to hunt with his head up, on the wind, instead of on the ground, and to effect a stylish and attractive carriage.

Let it be borne in mind that all of the foregoing instructions are intended for young dogs or puppies, as a primary course of learning, commonly known as yard-breaking, and they should be instilled with a view of relieving the master or sportsman of much work on the pup's début in the field. Remember that he should be drilled under them until he is taken to the outer world for work and business. Kind treatment is the rule, and mild measures should be adopted from the first; with firmness, patience, and perseverance, success is assured. Endeavor to impress upon your dog the fact that you are his master and not he yours; that you are his friend, and, though ever ready to supply his wants, and reward him for his good deeds, you are equally resolved to punish his transgressions.

Some authors on breaking advise — if the shooting season finds your pup six months old — taking him into the field without any previous instructions, assuring you that the work of training can be accomplished with half the labor necessary in the yard, or out of season. I most emphatically differ from them on this point, and think that the want of practical knowledge which such advice evinces is glaringly apparent. I do not deny that a dog can be broken in the field without any previous preparation, nor contend that yard-breaking is absolutely necessary to make a fielder. I do know, however, that first lessons in the field are attended with innumerable difficulties, and I would advise you to defer entering there, for a month at least, for your pup's sake, delaying until he is familiar with a few signs and commands, which are intended to govern his actions when on game.

CHAPTER VI.

WE will now return for a time to the first months of pup's life, to give emphasis to several points of infinite importance, the consideration of which we have reserved to avoid confusion. At a very early age he should be accustomed to, and, in fact, taught to welcome, the sound of the gun. If this essential in his training is neglected until the time when he should enter the field, deplorable results very often follow. Not infrequently a dog is rendered absolutely worthless by the terrible fright experienced when a gun is first fired over or near him. In fact, a pup should, in as much as possible, be accustomed to every unusual sound. But if he can stand without flinching while a gun is fired within a few feet of him, it is unlikely that other sounds will cause him excessive fright.

Almost every trainer has methods peculiarly his own by which he accustoms his pups to the

27

sound of the gun. All of value that are applied
at the early period of life are, however, based on
the same principle. They teach a pup to love a
gun, by associating with its discharge some espe-
cial pleasure. The primary measures which you
use are unimportant; a drum, if you have one, or
an old tin pan, or an empty box, will do, — something which, when struck with a stick, will emit
a sharp, quick sound. This you should at first
keep at a distance from the pup's kennel or pen.
When taking his food to him, whistle or call him
as is your wont, and at the same time give a
stroke on whatever you have selected, be it drum
or pan, and then rapidly approach and feed him.

Pursue this method, giving each day a heavier
stroke, and then, after a time, move the instrument which you employ nearer his kennel, lessen-
ing the distance gradually. He will in this way
associate the sounds with your coming, and also
with his food or his liberty, and, in time, no din
which you can make, even in his pen, will unnerve
him. Quite the reverse: he will gladly endure it
for the pleasure which he is certain will follow.

This much accomplished, it will be well for you
now to use a gun or pistol. Instead of the old

and familiar sound, let him hear you explode a cap at a distance, when you call to him. Follow the same methods of procedure as before, and each day bring the sound nearer, until at last the snapping of a cap over his head will fail to startle him. Now, instead of a cap, use a charge of powder. It should be light at first, and finally a full charge. If, in the same way advised, he is gradually accustomed to the sound of the gun, it will have no terrors for him; on the contrary, he will learn to love and welcome it.

During the employment of this system, it will be well to occasionally seek the aid of an assistant, who will fire while you are with the pup, and are closely watching him. If any evidence of fear is noted, you must lay aside the gun and return to the first method advised, and again pass through the different stages of the exercise.

This course which I have recommended is a conservative one. True, in some instances, if the gun is used from the first, and the pup is gradually accustomed to its sound, possibly the result will be the same. It might not be as well, however, for there is more or less danger in the method; while in the slower and more tedious process which I advised, success is almost fully assured, and no risk incurred.

While your pup is still young, there is one peculiarity which will need correction. Any setter or pointer will naturally chase cats or rabbits, and in the course of his education he must be broken from this. It ought not be difficult to soon teach him not to exhibit the objectionable trait. Almost every household has its cat; if not, it would be well to bring one up with the pup, that he may become thoroughly acquainted with her kind before he enters the field; otherwise, they will come in for a share of his attention. He should also be made familiar with rabbits, or he will be as likely to point, if not chase, them, as he would higher game. .A pair can easily be obtained, and for them quarters should be built near his pen, and connecting with it by a small opening. Through this they can pass at will, and in a short time become so well acquainted he will be utterly indifferent to them.

For the same obvious reasons you should accustom your pup to fowls. If you do not keep them, it will be of no little advantage for you to secure a pair; when possible, bring up a brood of chickens with him. If he is introduced to them while yet young, and attempts to chase and worry them, he is likely to soon encounter the mother and receive from her a rebuke which will prove effectual; and ever after he will treat her little ones with greater consideration.

In pursuance of this plan which we have outlined, it will be advisable for you to try and anticipate every contingency. While yet he is very young, you should familiarize your pup, in as much as possible, with the distracting influences which he is likely to encounter after his education has actually commenced.

There yet remains one point which, although seemingly trifling, still deserves mention. It is the need to habituate him to the restraint of the chain. The earlier this is done the better; for the difficulty increases with delay. As soon as it is apparent that he is capable of understanding, fasten a light chain to his collar, and then follow for a short time as he moves about, being careful not to resist him. In a few days he will become somewhat accustomed to it, and you can then begin to control his movements. The restraint must be very slight at first, however, and he should be coaxed, not forced, to follow you. Do not prolong the lesson, but let him learn gradually, and he will soon trot along by your side like an old dog.

You must now accustom him to greater restraint, and until he is taught to bear it patiently you will need to be firm in your conduct with him. Chain him up, and remain at first quieting his fears and lightening his hardship by kind words and caresses. When he no longer struggles, unchain and set him free. Repeat the lesson two or three times a day, leaving him alone after the first two or three days. You must observe this rule, namely: never release him while he still struggles and tugs at his chain. Resist his piteous appeals, and only free him when he becomes quiet. He will soon learn that struggling and howling are purposeless, and that complete submission to your wishes is the only course cpen to him.

We will now return and take up the trail where we left it, and introduce our rapidly maturing pup to the duties for which he was being prepared when we digressed to give you these hints on early management.

CHAPTER VII.

TAKING THE PUP AFIELD.

You are fortunate if the game season finds your dog at the age of seven or eight months, and he has learned the lessons which we have already assigned; you can now take him to the field while they are yet fresh in his mind. The change will be no less pleasing than bewildering; the scent which is emitted from the grouse and quail will tickle his nose more than the morsels of meat did his palate, and he will awake to a world of new sensations and delights. If he is a well bred puppy, in good health and courageous, he will at first probably be wild, and unmindful of everything said or done. Do not repress him at once, or restrain his dash and range, but permit him to run riot for an hour or two, when he will come down to his work. This eagerness is not objectionable in a youngster. It is indicative of physical vigor and good breeding, and, to a certain extent, is evidence that he possesses the essential qualities. It is advisable to take with you, when convenient, a good old steady dog; your young one will be apt to watch and follow after he has tired a little.

You must now be on the *qui vive* for his first stand or point; and when it occurs, or he shows signs of game, caution him with the command "Heed," uttered in a low, prolonged tone. Approach and flush the covey, and endeavor to bring down one bird at least. If pup rushes after the scattering brood, you must not be surprised or get angry. Remember that this is the prey he is bred to pursue, and one on which you threw him; he has not as yet been taught *not* to pursue it when it is trying to escape. You must cry "Down charge," and if he does not obey, go to him, get him by the collar, and bring him back to the spot where he pointed, and there make him "charge" while you reload. Then cast him off in the direction of the fallen bird, saying, "Dead! seek dead!" repeating these words until he finds it; then say, "Fetch, fetch!" If he should not pick up the bird at first, and fetch promptly, do not allow him to nose or mouth it, but take it up yourself, and apparently make much of it; stroke down the feathers, and allow him to smell and enjoy it while in your hand. Though he natu- rally wants it himself, he will soon learn, as he watches it go into the game-bag after every shot, that you want it also, and intend to claim it.

It is, of course, well to drop, if possible, a bird with each shot, so as to associate in the dog's mind the shooting with the possession of the cov- eted game; yet the killing of birds now must be a secondary consideration, and your whole atten- tion should be given to your pupil. For this reason it is well to have a companion to shoot and mark down game, while you have an eye exclusively to the pup. If he is wayward and perverse, I would suggest the use of a small, strong cord, about twenty feet long; this should be attached to his collar. When he comes to a point, approach him from behind and get hold of or put your foot on the same, and caution him with "Heed." Your comrade will now flush the birds, and pup in breaking shot will be jerked heels over head, perhaps, to the tune of "Down charge." It will require but a few such lessons to bring him to a sense of duty, to teach him to drop on the discharge of the gun. Whenever a bird is killed, after you have reloaded throw your dog off in the direction of dead game by a motion of your hand, saying, as before, "Dead seek," or "Seek dead." Continue on each occasion to urge him to "fetch"; this he will surely do sooner or later if he has been well trained in the yard.

Always approach the marked covey or bird to leeward, in order to give your dog every advantage of the scent, and to avoid blunders which he will be apt to make running down wind on his game. In the course of time, if hunted regularly, he will soon learn to fall down wind himself, and hold well up on it in the search. When you note that your dog does this, you can congratulate yourself upon the possession of a valuable hunter, and one which will only require work to bring him near perfection. After using the cord for a few days, you can take it off and give the pup a trial without it. You must be on the alert, for very likely, upon the first flush, feeling no check, he will imagine that you wanted him to go. If he does so after the command "Charge," you must catch him and use the lash, sparingly, however, at first.

CHAPTER VIII.

THE USE OF THE WHIP.

A FEW words regarding the whip. The sphere of its usefulness is a limited one, but for positive acts of disobedience and wilfulness it is necessary. An agent of good in the hands of a cool, resolute man, it becomes malignant when wielded on the impulse of a brutal mind. It is not the whip that has ruined so many dogs, but the man at the handle. The field is the place that calls for the most correction during the first and second seasons on game. Then, as a rule, the most gentle means should be resorted to, and those which have been employed in the yard should be applied. When, however, severe punishment is needed, there is nothing which can supply the place of the whip, and it should be used when a dog breaks shot, breaks his point, or wilfully disobeys. The sportsman should always go prepared with one that is strong and pliant, short, and easily carried in the pocket. The dog should never be threatened with it when about to be punished, but should be taken firmly by the collar with the left hand, his head held well down, and with the right hand the lash laid on. Then the whip should be slipped back into the pocket before the dog is let up. He painfully realizes the punishment received for his offence, and because he does not see the instrument used, he will be even more careful in his movements, lest he again invites such a woful and unaccountable experience. Never call a dog to you and whip him. Always go to him, or he will ever afterwards, when called, have his doubts as to what awaits him — whether the rawhide or a caress. On the other hand, when a dog is whipped at the place where he does wrong, he will ever after be only too glad to run to you when he is called, to keep you from going to him.

Let it be remembered that the foregoing precautions and rigid discipline are applicable to pups of very headstrong and perverse natures. Those that are timid should be handled very differently. They should be encouraged by reassuring words and your spirited manner while in the field. Animals are very quick to catch the habits and peculiarities of the associates with whom they are in daily contact. Strains differ very widely, too, in disposition and temperament. Some are predisposed to point stanchly at a very early age, are exceedingly tractable, and, withal, fearless; while others are almost unmanageable. I once owned a strain of pointers which, I have heard sportsmen say, the master deserved no credit for his training, for they were so very intelligent that only a few lessons were needed to prepare them for the field.

Continue your pup's education in the way which I was pointing out when we digressed to discuss the question of punishment. Make him now "down charge" on every shot, or stand until ordered on. Birds are often lying close after the first one rises on the wing. They would be flushed before you could reload, if your dog were allowed to break shot. Besides this, a dog should never be allowed to advance on game without a word or sign from his master. If such freedom is permitted under his eye, surely it will be taken when his back is turned, or the dog is out of his sight.

CHAPTER IX.

GUN-SHYNESS AND ITS CURE.

WE shall be obliged to linger at this point, and briefly discuss the subject of gun-shyness, which has always been one of exceeding interest for sportsmen. The theory that this peculiarity of disposition is inheritable has found many advocates, while some have dissented from it. There is no reason whatever why it should not be accepted as true; for there is a physiological law fixed and unalterable that both physical and mental peculiarities, be they imparted by inheritance, or acquired accidentally by faulty management in early life, are alike transmissible.

While, then, gun-shyness in a pup may be an inherent defect, testimony is not wanting to prove that it is by far more often due to incompetency, or criminal neglect, on the part of the trainer. No two puppies are alike in disposition; every gradation of courage is noted, not only in the different breeds but also in the same litter. One will need restraint, and possibly the whip; while, with another, only by the kindest treatment can his timidity be overcome.

I do not say that every pup wanting in courage can by judicious management be regenerated and made fearless; I do say, however, that as an undaunted spirit may be broken and its possessor become shrinking, cowardly, and worthless, so, too, may a timid pup, by wise, humane, and thoughtful methods, acquire a courage which will sustain him through years of usefulness.

I have already advised you of the proper course to pursue to accustom your pup to the sound of the gun. Rarely will the result be disappointing, and if failure does occur I can but feel that the fault will be in its application rather than in the system itself. It may be your misfortune, through some reason or other, to be, when the season opens, the unhappy possessor of a gun-shy pup. A work of this character would scarcely be complete were this contingency unprovided for, and advice as to management is herein given.

We come now to a point where we are beset with many difficulties; there is scarcely any subject which interests sportsmen, on which there is a greater diversity of opinion. With this fact those who have watched the kennel press for the past ten years are familiar. In articles on gun-shyness which have appeared in the "American Field" it is noted that while one claims that the defect is a fatal one, another is equally sure that it is curable. One writer considers two distinct forms of gun-shyness, namely: natural, or hereditary; and unnatural, or induced by circumstances, — the former he deems incurable. This theory is certainly ingenious, but reason can scarcely sustain such a nicety of distinction, if we consider this fault of disposition only; that is, if a dog is simply terrorized by the sound of the gun, and yet shows no lack of courage under other conditions. Here, again, we find ourselves dealing with the improbable; for by far the largest proportion of gun-shy dogs are, under all circumstances in which courage is needed, notably deficient in that attribute. If a young dog, nearing maturity, is of a skulking, cowardly nature, it will be next to impossible to instil into him the quality in which he is so essentially lacking, and, very properly, such an unfortunate should be condemned as incurable. If, however, he can encounter the ordinary experiences of life without fear, and the sound of the gun alone causes excessive fright, then there are many chances in his favor, and a cure may, under judicious management, be expected. There is truth in what one sportsman has said: "I would a thousand times rather own a gun-shy dog that had plenty of nerve and hunt in him when without a gun, than a timid one that was not gun-shy."

A variety of methods for the treatment of gun-shyness have been recommended. As is the case in many physical disturbances, a measure which may be efficacious in one patient may prove valueless when administered to another. Some have advised taking a dog into the field and firing one hundred and fifty to two hundred shots near him; the object being to partially deafen him, and so diminish his sensitiveness. This method scarcely recommends itself.

Over some young dogs, those older and well trained have a decided influence, and if they are taken out day after day together, the former being securely held with a long cord so he cannot run, and otherwise unnoticed, the fault may be overcome. Generally this method is soon abandoned as too sore a tax upon the trainer.

The treatment which promises the best results is a modification of that course advised for accustoming puppies to the sound of the gun. Chain your dog up and every time you feed him, stand where he can see you, but at some distance from him, and then fire. With the gun still in your hand, approach rapidly and feed him. It will be well, while submitting him to this discipline, to give less than the usual quantity of food, that he may be more anxious for it. Fire the gun every time you visit his kennel, and always follow the explosion with some special pleasure for him — either a dainty morsel to eat, or his liberty. Lessen the distance from which you fire each day, but do it very gradually.

Be observing, and watch the effect of this treatment; some slight modifications may be necessary. The course advised necessitates some trouble, and, as in all branches of dog training, patience will be indispensable. I do not claim that in every instance by following this system you will be successful; but I insist that it will prove effective much oftener than it will fail, and moreover it is the one among them all which promises the best results. If after giving it a fair trial your dog is still terrorized by the gun, you will have good reason to feel that the case is well nigh hopeless.

Before leaving this subject, a word upon the permanency of the cure of gun-shyness. Many will tell you that the fault, while seemingly overcome, is yet liable to reappear. This tendency, of course, may exist for a time, and unusual care and watchfulness will be needed to combat it. In time, however, the owner may feel reasonably secure against the return of the trouble.

CHAPTER X.

THE SECRET OF SUCCESSFUL TRAINING.

HAVING worked your dog for a part of the season, you should withdraw his older companion, so as not to engender a feeling of dependency. Take him into open, scant fields, with cover further removed, in order to bring out his ranging qualities, which are all desirable, and even indispensable, in a field dog. I hold that a well bred dog — one born of trained parents, and naturally fascinated with the odor of game — will perfect himself in this branch of service independently of all the rules which man can devise, providing, of course, he is regularly worked. Nature plays an important part in this matter, and it is only necessary to shape the tendencies with which she has endowed your pupil. It is well to accustom your dog to the motions of your hand, by which you will indicate the direction in which you wish him to go. When he is ordered on, you should always move in the same direction. When the game is marked down, you have the advantage of your dog, and he should be induced or forced to follow the course you direct. At other times, he has the advantage over you, in an organ of sense which enables him to discover where game is concealed.

On entering a field throw him off with a movement of your hand — to the right or left, as you may see fit. On his approach to a fence, cry " Heed," or " Ware fence," and whistle to attract his attention ; then cast him off again with another motion, and move in the same direction ; continue to do this until the whole field is drawn. Make him skirt and closely trim hedges, where game is often hid ; the heavy cover holds the scent, and it does not reach him at a distance. After two or three seasons' good work, a dog learns from experience to note the grounds and cover which are favorable to game, with as much accuracy as does his master ; and then it behooves the sportsman to let him have pretty much his own way on entering a new field ; for he is now well taught, and requires little or no assistance.

You will find that the secret of success in breaking a dog for service and the rôle of field companion is in following him up closely and encouraging him with your presence. Let him be assured by your actions and zeal that you are thoroughly in earnest, and never under any circumstances leave the field to return home, or go elsewhere, without giving him timely notice, or calling him in. Then by your conduct he will be assured of your kindly intentions. At the termination of every hunt, whistle him up, take off your game-bag, empty out the contents before him, let him see what you have both accomplished, and, while you put the birds back one by one, use endearing terms to him, laugh and make merry with him, appearing to be proud of your success; he will catch the spirit, and be no less pleased. All of this is flattering to him, and, though a youngster may not understand it at first, an old one fully appreciates it. I have owned old pointers who on occasions have seemed greatly overcome with joy, evincing it by rolling over and over, and jumping upon me and my gun, showing as much satisfaction and conceit as one can well imagine.

Mr. Edward Laverack, the famous old English breeder, says: — "I seldom use whip or whistle,

but allow my dogs to use their own natural sa-
gacity in making their casts and finding game. I
have ever found those dogs which range wide
turn out the best. It does not follow because a
dog ranges wide that he will not range close.
Where game is plentiful, a wide-ranging dog
must necessarily become a close ranger, because
here the game stops him ; it is high courage and
anxiety to find game that causes him to range
wide. A wide-ranging dog, too, saves you a
great deal of walking. Every shooting man
knows that he may occasionally tramp over two
or three miles without coming across anything ;
here it is, then, that a wide-ranging dog is of
greater utility than a close ranger."

CHAPTER XI.

QUARTERING is a most desirable qualification, and, when properly and well done, constitutes beautiful work. It is simply the movements of a dog on parallel lines over a field, cutting it up, as it were, and covering nearly all parts of it. The following diagram will explain the course both the sportsman and his dog should pursue in beating up game in an open field. The straight lines represent the direction the dog should go; the diagonal lines mark the course for the sportsman.

A represents the point from which the dog is thrown off in the direction of B, while the sportsman walks towards I, which point brings him in sufficient proximity to his dog when he reaches the fence or boundary to call him round on the next parallel line, C D, and while the dog is working down this, he walks from I to J, and so on, until the field is drawn. Of course a dog is not expected to describe perfectly straight lines, but if he even approximates them he will command all the game in the region through which

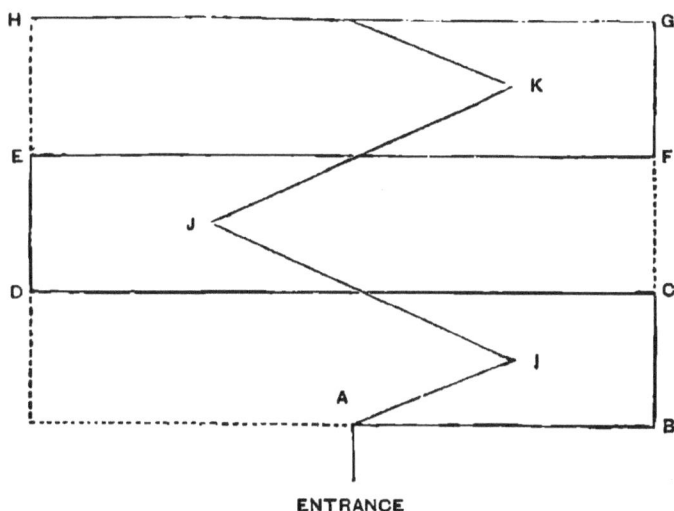

ENTRANCE

he passes. He should always be cast off with a motion of the hand, and the command "Hie away." At the points where the straight and diagonal lines approach each other, and where it is supposed he will pass in front of you, the words, "Hie away," "Hunt for it," or other familiar expressions of encouragement, should be used, but in a low tone of voice, for fear of startling hidden game.

Backing is another very necessary qualification, and it is simply the act of one dog in coming to a

stand the moment he sees another on a point.
Although the attitudes of dogs at a point and at
a back are similar, — the one, possibly, more mo-
tionless and fixed than the other, — there is a distinction. A point is when a dog stands at the
scent of game; a back is when he stands another
dog — in other words, he realizes the situation,
and fears to move lest he disturb and flush the
game which his brace-mate is holding. This, I
think, is acquired in most instances from associa-
tion, although I have seen many young dogs back
instinctively, but they were of strains the innate
tractable qualities of which were very notable.
It so often occurs that a youngster runs up by the
side of an older dog on his point, and stands at
the scent, that it is but reasonable to suppose
that in the course of time he learns to associate
the presence of game with the attitude of his
comrade; he cautiously approaches, and eventu-
ally backs him regardless of distance. Now, in
order to train a young dog which seems averse to
backing, or persists in rushing up to the scent,
my plan is to command him softly to "heed" —
which means that he must stop — when I know
he sees the dog pointing. If he has been made to

obey this command before, he will, of course, do so now. Then I go before him in a cautious, creeping posture, to impress him by my own actions that there is game ahead, making him keep his position until I flush and fire. This constant practice will ultimately bring him to a sense of his duty. If, on repeated occasions like this, your dog persists in running in and flushing game across the nose of his mate or companion, you must catch him in the act, and then thrash him soundly. Be quick, that he may know the cause of his punishment, and I will warrant that in a short time he will move up with more caution, and prove a backer in the end.

CHAPTER XII.

A POINT is now reached where, in a rambling way at least, we may properly discuss certain subjects which have an important bearing upon the one which we have been treating. It is believed by some, possibly many, that the mouthing of a bird lessens, in a certain degree, the power of scent; that it impairs that nicety of nose which is so essential when game is scarce or lying close. The advocates of this theory, therefore, discourage retrieving, and decline to teach their dogs this accomplishment, which their opponents, on the contrary, consider of very great importance. At least, those who find it impossible to keep more than one or a brace of dogs must consider in them the qualities of a retriever invaluable, and we might say indispensable. I have serious doubts if mouthing affects the nose, since there are so many instances where dogs have pointed game with their dead birds in the mouth.

If they can do this under these circumstances, how much less pernicious must be the influences, if any, which remain after birds have been dropped from the mouth, and the dog has again sought the wind.   There is another factor to be considered ; it does not seem impossible (far from it; it is more than probable) that a dog would lose heart and run with less spirit were he restrained on every occasion from approaching the game which he sees fall to his work, while an idler at the heels of his master is allowed the honor of retrieving what he was in no way instrumental in securing.

It is believed that a dog constantly improves until six years old.   As each intervening year passes, he feels more keenly his sense of duty; his attachments become firmer, and he is more deeply impressed with the fact that upon his actions his master's success in the field very greatly depends.   In considering the qualities which are essential in a dog, a good nose is, of course, first in importance.   Endowed by Nature, it is to him what genius is to the artist, the sculptor.   All other qualities may be acquired, but this must be inborn.   Staunchness and tractability may be said to come next on the list, and these three qualities may be considered the cardinal virtues. Scarcely less desirable is endurance, which some breeds of dogs naturally possess in a greater degree than others; all in good health and physically well developed may, however, acquire it under a judicious system of training. Style and dash are to a very great extent gifts by inheritance. The same may be said of speed and range, which are yet largely propagated by cultivation; the former, it is true, is not as requisite in the setter and pointer as in some other breeds of sporting dogs. We have already discussed retrieving and estimated its value.

The question of superiority between the pointer and setter is one on which sportsmen are at variance, and it doubtless will ever remain unsettled excepting in individual minds. It may be fairly said that there is but little to choose between the two for field work. Some consider that the pointer is the setter's equal under all conditions; the latter is, however, better fitted for low countries, abounding in lakes and marshes, and he is, I think, less sensitive to cold. In the upland, hilly, and undulating portions of the

South, the winter season finds the fields an inter-
minable waste of cockle-burs.   These are too
well known to every sportsman to require any
description.   The slightest brush is sufficient to
detach them from their stems ; they are, therefore, a source of exceeding annoyance to setters,
becoming entangled as they do in their long hair,
from which they are only removed with the great-
est difficulty.   Not infrequently these dogs, on
a hot trail, will stop and attempt to pull out the
pests from their coats with their teeth.   In such
countries the pointer is but slightly inconveni-
enced, and he needs but a brush through the bush
or stiff cover to remove the burs if they have
attached themselves to him.

Setters and pointers have ever seemed to divide
the honors, and there is one breed of dogs, hardy
workers — the cocker spaniels — of which very
little is generally known.   Oftentimes the briers
and bushes are so thick, the size of the pointer,
or his reluctance to enter, or the thick long hair
of the setter, is the cause of a light, or empty,
game-bag.   Under such conditions, the cocker is
invaluable.   Never over twelve inches high, lithe
and ambitious, he can easily penetrate and pass

through cover which to the larger dog is impassable. The assertion that this breed of dogs is unfitted to endure the fatigue of hunting is disproved by those who own them. Quick, alert, strong, and handsome little animals are the genuine cockers, and, withal, as intelligent, affectionate, and tractable dogs as are bred. This is the testimony of their admirers, and there is no reason to feel that it is an exaggeration.

CHAPTER XIII.

CONCLUSION.

"The little handful of things that I know" have been pulled up in the field behind incomparable dogs, made so by the same methods of teaching which I have suggested in the foregoing chapters. Long experience has taught me their value, and justified my recommending them to the reader. I trust that he will recognize their simplicity.

All men are not equally endowed by Nature with the qualities essential to a successful trainer. Truth sustains the satirist who wrote that there are certain men who could never train a dog with all the instruction and experience of a lifetime; and there are others who cannot handle a dog without ruining it, even after it is trained.

Some train their dogs in a way that is almost inexplicable; they themselves can scarcely tell you how they attain the desired result. Such men are invariably very quiet, unobtrusive, and self-reliant. They are also closely observant, great lovers of Nature's works, and possess a keen relish for the pleasures of the field.

Dog training may not improperly be considered an art. To practise it successfully, a great degree of patience, and at least an ordinary amount of intelligence, are demanded. Some pups are quick to learn, and are easily controlled; with these, the trainer has comparatively little or no trouble. There are many, however, more or less wayward and perverse, which will sorely tax his patience, and, to succeed with them, he must use great tact, perseverance, and firmness. A thorough knowledge of the pupil's sire and dam, their peculiarities, temperament, qualifications, etc., will materially aid a trainer in his work of instruction.

I have purposely omitted advice as to the care of dogs, such as feeding, exercise, kenneling, etc. Those subjects are fully treated of in works devoted to general management, and need not be herein considered. It will be necessary for you to teach your pup decorum, that he must not be familiar with strangers; possibly, too, you may be obliged to overcome his fear of water. These trifling matters have not been dwelt upon, as they will naturally suggest themselves to the intelligent student, and certainly none other ought to undertake the tuition of a pup.

In conclusion, the earnest hope is expressed that, in the duty he assumes, the amateur trainer will study Nature, and endeavor to assist her; that he will try to interpret rightly her promptings, and seek to educate his pupil by guiding and shaping his instinctive tendencies, rather than attempt to fix by force the principles he would have him acquire.

ASHMONT KENNELS

OF

THOROUGHBRED ENGLISH MASTIFFS.

This is the most noted Kennel of the breed in America.

It was here that the largest pair of Mastiffs on record were bred.

Weight of ASHMONT NERO, when thirteen and one-half months old, 190 pounds; that of his litter sister, LORNA DOONE, 2d, at the same age, 165 pounds.

Puppies out of the most noted dogs of the day always for sale.

Address,

ASHMONT KENNELS,

1101 TREMONT STREET, BOSTON, MASS.

www.ingramcontent.com/pod-product-compliance
Lightning Source LLC
Chambersburg PA
CBHW021524090426

42739CB00007B/767